# Dream Life
## every day

$\sim\!\infty\!\sim$

# 30 DAYS
*to*
## AUDACIOUS JOY AND
## LIVING A LIFE YOU LOVE

# DENISE WALSH

DREAM LIFE EVERY DAY by Denise Walsh
1006 Cherry St SE
Grand Rapids, MI 49506
DeniseWalsh.com
hello@denisewalsh.com

Unless otherwise noted, Scripture quotations are taken from the Holy Bible, New International Version®, NIV®. Copyright © 1973, 1978, 1984, 2011 by Biblica, Inc.™ Used by permission of Zondervan. All rights reserved worldwide. www.zondervan.com The "NIV" and "New International Version" are trademarks registered in the United States Patent and Trademark Office by Biblica, Inc.™

Scripture quotations marked NLT are from the Holy Bible, New Living Translation, copyright © 2007. Used by permission of Tyndale House Publishers, Inc., Wheaton, IL 60189. All rights reserved.

Visit the author's website at DeniseWalsh.com.

International Standard Book Number: 978-0-692-15614-8

19 20 21 22 23 — 9 8 7 6 5 4 3 2
Printed in the United States of America

# Introduction

> God gave us the gift of life; it
> is up to us to give ourselves
> the gift of living well.
>
> Voltaire

Your dream life is within your reach. It is not some intangible, far-off wish. It is the guaranteed end result of a journey that includes careful planning, consistent action, and the right attitude. That planning, that action, and that attitude begin now.

People often assume that persistence is the mind-set that most contributes to success, but that's not entirely correct. You cannot have clarity about where you're going in life—nor will you reach that destination—until you are able to embrace where you are today. Until you cultivate an attitude of gratefulness for the life you have already, you will not be able pursue your best life freely. Over the next thirty days, this journal will help you shift your focus so that you can chase your goals instead of merely running to escape your current reality.

Beginning your morning with this attitude of gratitude, as well as prayer, meditation, reflection, and a plan of action, will help you to get centered so that you can pursue your dream life from a place of clarity and a place of peace. Like all the journals in this series, *Dream Life Every Day* contains a series of not-so obvious exercises that will help you start your day right and bring you closer to creating the life that accomplishes all of your goals. If you will spend twenty to thirty minutes on this each day, you'll learn how to create the space you need to first set your mind and heart and then make an action plan to ensure that each day is productive.

Over the course of this thirty-day journey, there will be lots of repetition. You will rewrite your goal daily. You will rewrite and repeat life-changing affirmations daily. You will make time each day to be thankful for the life you have and to picture in vivid detail the life you dream of. This is intentional. It takes twenty-one days to form a habit, and the goal here is to establish new habits and turn those practices into a lifestyle that will breed success. Resist the urge to skip these exercises because they are the same as what you did the day before. Trust me; taking the time to choose joy now and to cement your dream by visualizing it vividly on a daily basis will bring you closer and closer to achieving it. You are creating new thought patterns and strengthening your identity, so consistency is key.

If, as you begin this journey, you discover that you need help connecting your big dreams with specific action items, or if you need to learn how to dream big and set actionable goals for the first time, visit DeniseWalsh.com. There you'll find other resources that work in tandem with this journal to give you a step-by-step pathway toward your best life and lay a foundation for the pursuit of your passion.

My dream is for you to feel immense joy and live your Dream Life in every way, every day! That takes both a decision to begin this journey and your commitment to an ongoing growth process. Make this journal part of your morning routine, and it will serve as a daily action guide that will give you a space to grow personally, keep you on track, allow you to see real progress, help you reach that elusive next level, and break through whatever ceiling is holding you back.

It's time for you to enjoy the journey, my friends. Enjoy today!

# Day 1

Our greatest glory is not in never falling, but in rising every time we fall.

Confucius

# Morning Prayer

Thank You, God, for Your amazing power and work within my life. I see all that You orchestrate in my life and am grateful for Your influence. I am grateful for the people, the opportunities, and the experiences that are placed on my path. I will take bold steps to live out Your purpose in my life today. I am accomplishing my dreams and have joy within my heart. Thank You for the explosion of goodness today as I live fully engaged, with my heart and my eyes wide open to You. I choose to see You work within my life today and every day.

# Eyes Wide Open

Take a few moments to consider how God has made His presence known in your life lately. What prayers has He answered for you? How have you experienced Him in your life or surroundings?

_____

_____

_____

_____

_____

_____

# Gratitude Game
## It's a Great Day for a Great Day

What are your favorite things about your life right now? What makes them so special to you?

# Prayer Requests

This is a special place of hope, victory, and healing. It is your opportunity to ask the Holy Spirit to move in certain situations and relationships. Rather than filing your complaints, tell Him how you'd like these situations and relationships to look. Jot down four specific requests below, being careful to focus on asking Him for victory in these areas instead of simply listing grievances. Be sure to pay attention over time to how things change.

1 _____

_____

_____

2 _____

_____

_____

3 _____

_____

_____

4 _____

_____

_____

# Meditation

You asked the Holy Spirit to move. Now listen for God's voice. You can add music or keep it silent. Make a goal to add more time to this section over the coming weeks.

# Reflection

During your time of meditation, did you sense God speaking to you? What do you believe He is calling you to do? Do you feel excited? Conflicted? Peaceful? Was anyone brought to your mind? Did you get a new idea? Now is the time to write it all down!

_____

_____

_____

_____

_____

_____

_____

_____

_____

_____

_____

_____

_____

_____

_____

_____

_____

# My Current Dream Life Goal

Writing your goal down each and every day creates momentum over time. Use this space to write down the Dream Life goal or other big goal you are working toward.

_____

_____

_____

# Affirmations

Daily affirmations are simple, positive statements declaring specific goals in their completed state. To get started, think about who you will be, how you will feel, and what your life will look like when your goal is complete. Then write several statements that agree with this outcome. A few examples are: I am a supportive and loving spouse and an engaged parent. I happily love myself exactly the way I am. I am earning $4,000 a month or more.

When you are done, read these affirmations out loud to yourself. You will do this every day until you truly believe it and then embody it.

**I am** _____

**I am** _____

**I am** _____

**I am** _____

# Visualization

Cement your Dream Life goal in your mind by picturing yourself achieving it. What will your life look like when your goal is completed? Notice any new details you can see today.

# Dream Life Goal Action Items:

This to-do list is not about laundry, groceries, or baths for the kids. These are action-oriented steps for today that will move you toward your goal. Make sure they are all small enough to accomplish and check off your list today.

These action items should also be specific. For example, "work on project" is not specific enough, because your project might take weeks to complete. Break it down into pieces, such as "work on chapter 1," "call ten prospects," or "join a local meet-up group."

☐ _____

☐ _____

☐ _____

# Dream Health Action Item:

List one health-conscious thing you plan to do today. Is it to improve your water intake? Make more time for exercise? Tweak your menu or your sleep time?

☐ _____

# Dream Relationship Action Items:

What can you do today to be more intentional about important relationships? Text your spouse? Connect with a friend? Plan special times with each of your children?

☐ _____

☐ _____

☐ _____

☐ _____

# Day 2

All our dreams can come true, if we
have the courage to pursue them.

Walt Disney

# Morning Prayer

Thank You, God, for Your amazing power and work within my life. I see all that You orchestrate in my life and am grateful for Your influence. I am grateful for the people, the opportunities, and the experiences that are placed on my path. I will take bold steps to live out Your purpose in my life today. I am accomplishing my dreams and have joy within my heart. Thank You for the explosion of goodness today as I live fully engaged, with my heart and my eyes wide open to You. I choose to see You work within my life today and every day.

# Eyes Wide Open

Take a few moments to consider how God has made His presence known in your life lately. What prayers has He answered for you? How have you experienced Him in your life or surroundings?

_____

_____

_____

_____

_____

_____

# Gratitude Game
## Personal Talent Scout

Describe a special gift or talent you have, how you use it, and why you are grateful for it.

# Prayer Requests

This is a special place of hope, victory, and healing. It is your opportunity to ask the Holy Spirit to move in certain situations and relationships. Rather than filing your complaints, tell Him how you'd like these situations and relationships to look. Jot down four specific requests below, being careful to focus on asking Him for victory in these areas instead of simply listing grievances. Be sure to pay attention over time to how things change.

1 _____
_____
_____

2 _____
_____
_____

3 _____
_____
_____

4 _____
_____
_____

# Meditation

You asked the Holy Spirit to move. Now listen for God's voice. You can add music or keep it silent. Make a goal to add more time to this section over the coming weeks.

*Dream Life Every Day*

# Reflection

Did you sense God speaking to you? What do you believe
He is calling you to do? Do you feel excited? Conflicted?
Peaceful? Was anyone brought to your mind? Did you get a
new idea? Now is the time to write it all down!

_____

_____

_____

_____

_____

_____

_____

_____

_____

_____

_____

_____

_____

_____

_____

_____

_____

_____

# Dream Life Goal

Writing your goal down each and every day creates momentum over time. Use this space to write down the Dream Life goal or other big goal you are working toward.

_____

_____

_____

_____

_____

# Affirmations

Who will you be, how will you feel, and what will your life look like when your goal is complete? Write down the affirmations that correspond to the person you are becoming and the life you are creating. When you are done, read these affirmations out loud to yourself.

**I am** _____

**I am** _____

**I am** _____

**I am** _____

**I am** _____

# Visualization

Cement your big goal in your mind by picturing yourself achieving it. What will your life look like when your goal is completed? Notice any new details you can see today.

# Dream Life Goal Action Items:

Remember, this to-do list is not about laundry, groceries, or baths for the kids. These are action-oriented steps for today that will move you toward your goal. Make sure they are all small enough and specific enough to accomplish and check off your list today.

- ☐ _____
- ☐ _____
- ☐ _____
- ☐ _____
- ☐ _____

# Dream Health Action Item:

List one health-conscious thing you plan to do today. Is it to improve your water intake? Make more time for exercise? Tweak your menu or your sleep time?

- ☐ _____

# Dream Relationship Action Items:

What can you do today to be more intentional about important relationships? Text your spouse? Connect with a friend? Plan special times with each of your children?

- ☐ _____
- ☐ _____
- ☐ _____
- ☐ _____

# Day 3

Today is life—the only life you are sure of. Make the most of today. Get interested in something. Shake yourself awake. Develop a hobby. Let the winds of enthusiasm sweep through you. Live today with gusto.

Dale Carnegie

# Morning Prayer

Thank You, God, for Your amazing power and work within my life. I see all that You orchestrate in my life and am grateful for Your influence. I am grateful for the people, the opportunities, and the experiences that are placed on my path. I will take bold steps to live out Your purpose in my life today. I am accomplishing my dreams and have joy within my heart. Thank You for the explosion of goodness today as I live fully engaged, with my heart and my eyes wide open to You. I choose to see You work within my life today and every day.

# Eyes Wide Open

Take a few moments to consider how God has made His presence known in your life lately. What prayers has He answered for you? How have you experienced Him in your life or surroundings?

_____

_____

_____

_____

_____

_____

_____

# Gratitude Game

## Filled with Joy

List ten things that bring you joy.

1 _____

_____

2 _____

_____

3 _____

_____

4 _____

_____

5 _____

_____

6 _____

_____

7 _____

_____

8 _____

_____

9 _____

_____

10 _____

# Prayer Requests

This is a special place of hope, victory, and healing. It is your opportunity to ask the Holy Spirit to move in certain situations and relationships. Rather than filing your complaints, tell Him how you'd like these situations and relationships to look. Jot down four specific requests below, being careful to focus on asking Him for victory in these areas instead of simply listing grievances. Be sure to pay attention over time to how things change.

1 _____

_____

_____

2 _____

_____

_____

3 _____

_____

_____

4 _____

_____

_____

# Meditation

You asked the Holy Spirit to move. Now listen for God's voice. You can add music or keep it silent. Make a goal to add more time to this section over the coming weeks.

*Dream Life Every Day*

# Reflection

Did you sense God speaking to you? What do you believe He is calling you to do? Do you feel excited? Conflicted? Peaceful? Was anyone brought to your mind? Did you get a new idea? Now is the time to write it all down!

_____

_____

_____

_____

_____

_____

_____

_____

_____

_____

_____

_____

_____

_____

_____

_____

_____

# Dream Life Goal

Writing your goal down each and every day creates momentum over time. Use this space to write down the Dream Life goal or other big goal you are working toward.

_____

_____

_____

_____

_____

# Affirmations

Who will you be, how will you feel, and what will your life look like when your goal is complete? Write down the affirmations that correspond to the person you are becoming and the life you are creating. When you are done, read these affirmations out loud to yourself.

**I am** _____

**I am** _____

**I am** _____

**I am** _____

**I am** _____

# Visualization

Cement your big goal in your mind by picturing yourself achieving it. What will your life look like when your goal is completed? Notice any new details you can see today.

# Dream Life Goal Action Items:

Remember, this to-do list is not about laundry, groceries, or baths for the kids. These are action-oriented steps for today that will move you toward your goal. Make sure they are all small enough and specific enough to accomplish and check off your list today.

- ☐ _____
- ☐ _____
- ☐ _____
- ☐ _____
- ☐ _____

# Dream Health Action Item:

List one health-conscious thing you plan to do today. Is it to improve your water intake? Make more time for exercise? Tweak your menu or your sleep time?

- ☐ _____

# Dream Relationship Action Items:

What can you do today to be more intentional about important relationships? Text your spouse? Connect with a friend? Plan special times with each of your children?

- ☐ _____
- ☐ _____
- ☐ _____
- ☐ _____

# Day 4

Believe in yourself. You are braver than you think, more talented than you know, and capable of more than you imagine.

Roy T. Bennett

# Morning Prayer

Thank You, God, for Your amazing power and work within my life. I see all that You orchestrate in my life and am grateful for Your influence. I am grateful for the people, the opportunities, and the experiences that are placed on my path. I will take bold steps to live out Your purpose in my life today. I am accomplishing my dreams and have joy within my heart. Thank You for the explosion of goodness today as I live fully engaged, with my heart and my eyes wide open to You. I choose to see You work within my life today and every day.

# Eyes Wide Open

Take a few moments to consider how God has made His presence known in your life lately. What prayers has He answered for you? How have you experienced Him in your life or surroundings?

_____

_____

_____

_____

_____

_____

_____

# Gratitude Game

## Personal Award

Describe something you have done that you are particularly proud of. What about it makes you feel that way?

# Prayer Requests

This is a special place of hope, victory, and healing. It is your opportunity to ask the Holy Spirit to move in certain situations and relationships. Rather than filing your complaints, tell Him how you'd like these situations and relationships to look. Jot down four specific requests below, being careful to focus on asking Him for victory in these areas instead of simply listing grievances. Be sure to pay attention over time to how things change.

1 _____

_____

_____

2 _____

_____

_____

3 _____

_____

_____

4 _____

_____

_____

# Meditation

You asked the Holy Spirit to move. Now listen for God's voice. You can add music or keep it silent. Make a goal to add more time to this section over the coming weeks.

# Reflection

Did you sense God speaking to you? What do you believe He is calling you to do? Do you feel excited? Conflicted? Peaceful? Was anyone brought to your mind? Did you get a new idea? Now is the time to write it all down!

_Day 4_

# Dream Life Goal

Writing your goal down each and every day creates momentum over time. Use this space to write down the Dream Life goal or other big goal you are working toward.

_____

_____

_____

_____

_____

# Affirmations

Who will you be, how will you feel, and what will your life look like when your goal is complete? Write down the affirmations that correspond to the person you are becoming and the life you are creating. When you are done, read these affirmations out loud to yourself.

**I am** _____

**I am** _____

**I am** _____

**I am** _____

**I am** _____

# Visualization

Cement your big goal in your mind by picturing yourself achieving it. What will your life look like when your goal is completed? Notice any new details you can see today.

_Dream Life Every Day_

# Dream Life Goal Action Items:

Remember, this to-do list is not about laundry, groceries, or baths for the kids. These are action-oriented steps for today that will move you toward your goal. Make sure they are all small enough and specific enough to accomplish and check off your list today.

☐ _____

☐ _____

☐ _____

☐ _____

☐ _____

# Dream Health Action Item:

List one health-conscious thing you plan to do today. Is it to improve your water intake? Make more time for exercise? Tweak your menu or your sleep time?

☐ _____

# Dream Relationship Action Items:

What can you do today to be more intentional about important relationships? Text your spouse? Connect with a friend? Plan special times with each of your children?

☐ _____

☐ _____

☐ _____

☐ _____

# Day 5

When one door closes, another opens; but we often look so long and so regretfully upon the closed door that we do not see the one that has opened for us.

Alexander Graham Bell

# Morning Prayer

Thank You, God, for Your amazing power and work within my life. I see all that You orchestrate in my life and am grateful for Your influence. I am grateful for the people, the opportunities, and the experiences that are placed on my path. I will take bold steps to live out Your purpose in my life today. I am accomplishing my dreams and have joy within my heart. Thank You for the explosion of goodness today as I live fully engaged, with my heart and my eyes wide open to You. I choose to see You work within my life today and every day.

# Eyes Wide Open

Take a few moments to consider how God has made His presence known in your life lately. What prayers has He answered for you? How have you experienced Him in your life or surroundings?

_____

_____

_____

_____

_____

# Gratitude Game
## Always Growing

Write about a way that you have grown throughout the past year.

_____

_____

# Prayer Requests

This is a special place of hope, victory, and healing. It is your opportunity to ask the Holy Spirit to move in certain situations and relationships. Rather than filing your complaints, tell Him how you'd like these situations and relationships to look. Jot down four specific requests below, being careful to focus on asking Him for victory in these areas instead of simply listing grievances. Be sure to pay attention over time to how things change.

1 _____

_____

_____

2 _____

_____

_____

3 _____

_____

_____

4 _____

_____

_____

# Meditation

You asked the Holy Spirit to move. Now listen for God's voice. You can add music or keep it silent. Make a goal to add more time to this section over the coming weeks.

# Reflection

Did you sense God speaking to you? What do you believe He is calling you to do? Do you feel excited? Conflicted? Peaceful? Was anyone brought to your mind? Did you get a new idea? Now is the time to write it all down!

# Dream Life Goal

Writing your goal down each and every day creates momentum over time. Use this space to write down the Dream Life goal or other big goal you are working toward.

_____

_____

_____

_____

_____

_____

# Affirmations

Who will you be, how will you feel, and what will your life look like when your goal is complete? Write down the affirmations that correspond to the person you are becoming and the life you are creating. When you are done, read these affirmations out loud to yourself.

**I am** _____

**I am** _____

**I am** _____

**I am** _____

**I am** _____

# Visualization

Cement your big goal in your mind by picturing yourself achieving it. What will your life look like when your goal is completed? Notice any new details you can see today.

# Dream Life Goal Action Items:

Remember, this to-do list is not about laundry, groceries, or baths for the kids. These are action-oriented steps for today that will move you toward your goal. Make sure they are all small enough and specific enough to accomplish and check off your list today.

- [ ] _____
- [ ] _____
- [ ] _____
- [ ] _____
- [ ] _____

# Dream Health Action Item:

List one health-conscious thing you plan to do today. Is it to improve your water intake? Make more time for exercise? Tweak your menu or your sleep time?

- [ ] _____

# Dream Relationship Action Items:

What can you do today to be more intentional about important relationships? Text your spouse? Connect with a friend? Plan special times with each of your children?

- [ ] _____
- [ ] _____
- [ ] _____
- [ ] _____

# Day 6

Joy is the simplest form of gratitude.
Karl Barth

# Morning Prayer

Thank You, God, for Your amazing power and work within my life. I see all that You orchestrate in my life and am grateful for Your influence. I am grateful for the people, the opportunities, and the experiences that are placed on my path. I will take bold steps to live out Your purpose in my life today. I am accomplishing my dreams and have joy within my heart. Thank You for the explosion of goodness today as I live fully engaged, with my heart and my eyes wide open to You. I choose to see You work within my life today and every day.

# Eyes Wide Open

Take a few moments to consider how God has made His presence known in your life lately. What prayers has He answered for you? How have you experienced Him in your life or surroundings?

_____

_____

_____

_____

_____

_____

_____

_____

# Gratitude Game

## Joy in the Journey

How will you choose to find joy in everything on your plate? Write down at least five reasons you are grateful for everything you get to do today. Then throughout all the daily tasks, to-dos, errands, and work time, take a deep breath and repeat, "I love that I get to do this today."

_____

_____

_____

_____

_____

_____

_____

_____

_____

_____

_____

_____

_____

_____

_____

_____

_____

_____

_____

_____

_____

*Day 6*

# Prayer Requests

This is a special place of hope, victory, and healing. It is your opportunity to ask the Holy Spirit to move in certain situations and relationships. Rather than filing your complaints, tell Him how you'd like these situations and relationships to look. Jot down four specific requests below, being careful to focus on asking Him for victory in these areas instead of simply listing grievances. Be sure to pay attention over time to how things change.

1 _____

_____

_____

2 _____

_____

_____

3 _____

_____

_____

4 _____

_____

_____

# Meditation

You asked the Holy Spirit to move. Now listen for God's voice. You can add music or keep it silent. Make a goal to add more time to this section over the coming weeks.

*Dream Life Every Day*

# Reflection

Did you sense God speaking to you? What do you believe He is calling you to do? Do you feel excited? Conflicted? Peaceful? Was anyone brought to your mind? Did you get a new idea? Now is the time to write it all down!

_____

_____

_____

_____

_____

_____

_____

_____

_____

_____

_____

_____

_____

_____

_____

_____

_____

_____

# Dream Life Goal

Writing your goal down each and every day creates momentum over time. Use this space to write down the Dream Life goal or other big goal you are working toward.

_____

_____

_____

_____

_____

_____

# Affirmations

Who will you be, how will you feel, and what will your life look like when your goal is complete? Write down the affirmations that correspond to the person you are becoming and the life you are creating. When you are done, read these affirmations out loud to yourself.

**I am** _____

**I am** _____

**I am** _____

**I am** _____

**I am** _____

# Visualization

Cement your big goal in your mind by picturing yourself achieving it. What will your life look like when your goal is completed? Notice any new details you can see today.

# Dream Life Goal Action Items:

Remember, this to-do list is not about laundry, groceries, or baths for the kids. These are action-oriented steps for today that will move you toward your goal. Make sure they are all small enough and specific enough to accomplish and check off your list today.

☐ _____

☐ _____

☐ _____

☐ _____

☐ _____

# Dream Health Action Item:

List one health-conscious thing you plan to do today. Is it to improve your water intake? Make more time for exercise? Tweak your menu or your sleep time?

☐ _____

# Dream Relationship Action Items:

What can you do today to be more intentional about important relationships? Text your spouse? Connect with a friend? Plan special times with each of your children?

☐ _____

☐ _____

☐ _____

☐ _____

# Day 7

If you believe it will work out, you'll see opportunities. If you believe it won't, you will see obstacles.

Wayne Dyer

# Morning Prayer

Thank You, God, for Your amazing power and work within my life. I see all that You orchestrate in my life and am grateful for Your influence. I am grateful for the people, the opportunities, and the experiences that are placed on my path. I will take bold steps to live out Your purpose in my life today. I am accomplishing my dreams and have joy within my heart. Thank You for the explosion of goodness today as I live fully engaged, with my heart and my eyes wide open to You. I choose to see You work within my life today and every day.

# Eyes Wide Open

Take a few moments to consider how God has made His presence known in your life lately. What prayers has He answered for you? How have you experienced Him in your life or surroundings?

_____

_____

_____

_____

_____

_____

# Gratitude Game
## Overflowing

Describe something that makes you happy and why. How will you try to be around that source of happiness or do that activity more often?

# Prayer Requests

This is a special place of hope, victory, and healing. It is your opportunity to ask the Holy Spirit to move in certain situations and relationships. Rather than filing your complaints, tell Him how you'd like these situations and relationships to look. Jot down four specific requests below, being careful to focus on asking Him for victory in these areas instead of simply listing grievances. Be sure to pay attention over time to how things change.

1 _____

_____

_____

2 _____

_____

_____

3 _____

_____

_____

4 _____

_____

_____

# Meditation

You asked the Holy Spirit to move. Now listen for God's voice. You can add music or keep it silent. Make a goal to add more time to this section over the coming weeks.

# Reflection

Did you sense God speaking to you? What do you believe He is calling you to do? Do you feel excited? Conflicted? Peaceful? Was anyone brought to your mind? Did you get a new idea? Now is the time to write it all down!

_____

_____

_____

_____

_____

_____

_____

_____

_____

_____

_____

_____

_____

_____

_____

_____

_____

_____

_____

# Dream Life Goal

Writing your goal down each and every day creates momentum over time. Use this space to write down the Dream Life goal or other big goal you are working toward.

_____

_____

_____

_____

_____

# Affirmations

Who will you be, how will you feel, and what will your life look like when your goal is complete? Write down the affirmations that correspond to the person you are becoming and the life you are creating. When you are done, read these affirmations out loud to yourself.

**I am** _____

**I am** _____

**I am** _____

**I am** _____

**I am** _____

# Visualization

Cement your big goal in your mind by picturing yourself achieving it. What will your life look like when your goal is completed? Notice any new details you can see today.

*Dream Life Every Day*

# Dream Life Goal Action Items:

Remember, this to-do list is not about laundry, groceries, or baths for the kids. These are action-oriented steps for today that will move you toward your goal. Make sure they are all small enough and specific enough to accomplish and check off your list today.

- ☐ _____
- ☐ _____
- ☐ _____
- ☐ _____
- ☐ _____

# Dream Health Action Item:

List one health-conscious thing you plan to do today. Is it to improve your water intake? Make more time for exercise? Tweak your menu or your sleep time?

- ☐ _____

# Dream Relationship Action Items:

What can you do today to be more intentional about important relationships? Text your spouse? Connect with a friend? Plan special times with each of your children?

- ☐ _____
- ☐ _____
- ☐ _____
- ☐ _____

# Day 8

Surround yourself only with people
who are going to take you higher.
Oprah Winfrey

# Morning Prayer

Thank You, God, for Your amazing power and work within my life. I see all that You orchestrate in my life and am grateful for Your influence. I am grateful for the people, the opportunities, and the experiences that are placed on my path. I will take bold steps to live out Your purpose in my life today. I am accomplishing my dreams and have joy within my heart. Thank You for the explosion of goodness today as I live fully engaged, with my heart and my eyes wide open to You. I choose to see You work within my life today and every day.

# Eyes Wide Open

Take a few moments to consider how God has made His presence known in your life lately. What prayers has He answered for you? How have you experienced Him in your life or surroundings?

_____

_____

_____

_____

_____

_____

_____

# Gratitude Game

## BFF

Name someone you know who makes your life better and why. How could you be that for someone else today?

# Prayer Requests

This is a special place of hope, victory, and healing. It is your opportunity to ask the Holy Spirit to move in certain situations and relationships. Rather than filing your complaints, tell Him how you'd like these situations and relationships to look. Jot down four specific requests below, being careful to focus on asking Him for victory in these areas instead of simply listing grievances. Be sure to pay attention over time to how things change.

1 _____

_____

_____

2 _____

_____

_____

3 _____

_____

_____

4 _____

_____

_____

# Meditation

You asked the Holy Spirit to move. Now listen for God's voice. You can add music or keep it silent. Make a goal to add more time to this section over the coming weeks.

*Dream Life Every Day*

# Reflection

Did you sense God speaking to you? What do you believe He is calling you to do? Do you feel excited? Conflicted? Peaceful? Was anyone brought to your mind? Did you get a new idea? Now is the time to write it all down!

_____

_____

_____

_____

_____

_____

_____

_____

_____

_____

_____

_____

_____

_____

_____

_____

_____

_____

_____

# Dream Life Goal

Writing your goal down each and every day creates momentum over time. Use this space to write down the Dream Life goal or other big goal you are working toward.

_____

_____

_____

_____

_____

# Affirmations

Who will you be, how will you feel, and what will your life look like when your goal is complete? Write down the affirmations that correspond to the person you are becoming and the life you are creating. When you are done, read these affirmations out loud to yourself.

**I am** _____

**I am** _____

**I am** _____

**I am** _____

**I am** _____

# Visualization

Cement your big goal in your mind by picturing yourself achieving it. What will your life look like when your goal is completed? Notice any new details you can see today.

*Dream Life Every Day*

# Dream Life Goal Action Items:

Remember, this to-do list is not about laundry, groceries, or baths for the kids. These are action-oriented steps for today that will move you toward your goal. Make sure they are all small enough and specific enough to accomplish and check off your list today.

☐ _____

☐ _____

☐ _____

☐ _____

☐ _____

# Dream Health Action Item:

List one health-conscious thing you plan to do today. Is it to improve your water intake? Make more time for exercise? Tweak your menu or your sleep time?

☐ _____

# Dream Relationship Action Items:

What can you do today to be more intentional about important relationships? Text your spouse? Connect with a friend? Plan special times with each of your children?

☐ _____

☐ _____

☐ _____

☐ _____

# Day 9

The LORD will guide you always; he will satisfy your needs.

Isaiah 58:11

# Morning Prayer

Thank You, God, for Your amazing power and work within my life. I see all that You orchestrate in my life and am grateful for Your influence. I am grateful for the people, the opportunities, and the experiences that are placed on my path. I will take bold steps to live out Your purpose in my life today. I am accomplishing my dreams and have joy within my heart. Thank You for the explosion of goodness today as I live fully engaged, with my heart and my eyes wide open to You. I choose to see You work within my life today and every day.

# Eyes Wide Open

Take a few moments to consider how God has made His presence known in your life lately. What prayers has He answered for you? How have you experienced Him in your life or surroundings?

_____

_____

_____

_____

_____

_____

# Gratitude Game
## I Spy

Look around the room you're sitting in, or if you're not at home, picture yourself in your bedroom or living room. Find one thing that was gifted to you from someone you love. What makes that gift special to you?

*Dream Life Every Day*

# Prayer Requests

This is a special place of hope, victory, and healing. It is your opportunity to ask the Holy Spirit to move in certain situations and relationships. Rather than filing your complaints, tell Him how you'd like these situations and relationships to look. Jot down four specific requests below, being careful to focus on asking Him for victory in these areas instead of simply listing grievances. Be sure to pay attention over time to how things change.

**1** _____

_____

_____

**2** _____

_____

_____

**3** _____

_____

_____

**4** _____

_____

_____

# Meditation

You asked the Holy Spirit to move. Now listen for God's voice. You can add music or keep it silent. Make a goal to add more time to this section over the coming weeks.

*Dream Life Every Day*

# Reflection

Did you sense God speaking to you? What do you believe He is calling you to do? Do you feel excited? Conflicted? Peaceful? Was anyone brought to your mind? Did you get a new idea? Now is the time to write it all down!

_____

_____

_____

_____

_____

_____

_____

_____

_____

_____

_____

_____

_____

_____

_____

_____

_____

_____

_____

# Dream Life Goal

Writing your goal down each and every day creates momentum over time. Use this space to write down the Dream Life goal or other big goal you are working toward.

_____

_____

_____

_____

_____

# Affirmations

Who will you be, how will you feel, and what will your life look like when your goal is complete? Write down the affirmations that correspond to the person you are becoming and the life you are creating. When you are done, read these affirmations out loud to yourself.

**I am** _____

**I am** _____

**I am** _____

**I am** _____

**I am** _____

# Visualization

Cement your big goal in your mind by picturing yourself achieving it. What will your life look like when your goal is completed? Notice any new details you can see today.

# Dream Life Goal Action Items:

Remember, this to-do list is not about laundry, groceries, or baths for the kids. These are action-oriented steps for today that will move you toward your goal. Make sure they are all small enough and specific enough to accomplish and check off your list today.

- [ ] _____
- [ ] _____
- [ ] _____
- [ ] _____
- [ ] _____

# Dream Health Action Item:

List one health-conscious thing you plan to do today. Is it to improve your water intake? Make more time for exercise? Tweak your menu or your sleep time?

- [ ] _____

# Dream Relationship Action Items:

What can you do today to be more intentional about important relationships? Text your spouse? Connect with a friend? Plan special times with each of your children?

- [ ] _____
- [ ] _____
- [ ] _____
- [ ] _____

# Day 10

Success means doing the best we can with what we have. Success is the doing, not the getting; in the trying, not the triumph. Success is a personal standard, reaching for the highest that is in us, becoming all that we can be.

Zig Ziglar

# Morning Prayer

Thank You, God, for Your amazing power and work within my life. I see all that You orchestrate in my life and am grateful for Your influence. I am grateful for the people, the opportunities, and the experiences that are placed on my path. I will take bold steps to live out Your purpose in my life today. I am accomplishing my dreams and have joy within my heart. Thank You for the explosion of goodness today as I live fully engaged, with my heart and my eyes wide open to You. I choose to see You work within my life today and every day.

# Eyes Wide Open

Take a few moments to consider how God has made His presence known in your life lately. What prayers has He answered for you? How have you experienced Him in your life or surroundings?

_____

_____

_____

_____

_____

_____

_____

# Gratitude Game
## Weekly Review

Describe something that happened this past week that you are grateful for and why.

# Prayer Requests

This is a special place of hope, victory, and healing. It is your opportunity to ask the Holy Spirit to move in certain situations and relationships. Rather than filing your complaints, tell Him how you'd like these situations and relationships to look. Jot down four specific requests below, being careful to focus on asking Him for victory in these areas instead of simply listing grievances. Be sure to pay attention over time to how things change.

1 _____

_____

_____

2 _____

_____

_____

3 _____

_____

_____

4 _____

_____

_____

# Meditation

You asked the Holy Spirit to move. Now listen for God's voice. You can add music or keep it silent. Make a goal to add more time to this section over the coming weeks.

*Dream Life Every Day*

# Reflection

Did you sense God speaking to you? What do you believe He is calling you to do? Do you feel excited? Conflicted? Peaceful? Was anyone brought to your mind? Did you get a new idea? Now is the time to write it all down!

# Dream Life Goal

Writing your goal down each and every day creates momentum over time. Use this space to write down the Dream Life goal or other big goal you are working toward.

_____

_____

_____

_____

_____

_____

# Affirmations

Who will you be, how will you feel, and what will your life look like when your goal is complete? Write down the affirmations that correspond to the person you are becoming and the life you are creating. When you are done, read these affirmations out loud to yourself.

**I am** _____

**I am** _____

**I am** _____

**I am** _____

**I am** _____

# Visualization

Cement your big goal in your mind by picturing yourself achieving it. What will your life look like when your goal is completed? Notice any new details you can see today.

# Dream Life Goal Action Items:

Remember, this to-do list is not about laundry, groceries, or baths for the kids. These are action-oriented steps for today that will move you toward your goal. Make sure they are all small enough and specific enough to accomplish and check off your list today.

- [ ] _____
- [ ] _____
- [ ] _____
- [ ] _____
- [ ] _____

# Dream Health Action Item:

List one health-conscious thing you plan to do today. Is it to improve your water intake? Make more time for exercise? Tweak your menu or your sleep time?

- [ ] _____

# Dream Relationship Action Items:

What can you do today to be more intentional about important relationships? Text your spouse? Connect with a friend? Plan special times with each of your children?

- [ ] _____
- [ ] _____
- [ ] _____
- [ ] _____

# Day 11

If you set goals and go after them with all the determination you can muster, your gifts will take you places that will amaze you.

Les Brown

# Morning Prayer

Thank You, God, for Your amazing power and work within my life. I see all that You orchestrate in my life and am grateful for Your influence. I am grateful for the people, the opportunities, and the experiences that are placed on my path. I will take bold steps to live out Your purpose in my life today. I am accomplishing my dreams and have joy within my heart. Thank You for the explosion of goodness today as I live fully engaged, with my heart and my eyes wide open to You. I choose to see You work within my life today and every day.

# Eyes Wide Open

Take a few moments to consider how God has made His presence known in your life lately. What prayers has He answered for you? How have you experienced Him in your life or surroundings?

_____

_____

_____

_____

_____

_____

# Gratitude Game
## Precious Resources

What are your most valuable resources? Is it your time? Your education? Talents and skills? Finances? How can you use those resources to improve others' lives?

# Prayer Requests

This is a special place of hope, victory, and healing. It is your opportunity to ask the Holy Spirit to move in certain situations and relationships. Rather than filing your complaints, tell Him how you'd like these situations and relationships to look. Jot down four specific requests below, being careful to focus on asking Him for victory in these areas instead of simply listing grievances. Be sure to pay attention over time to how things change.

1 _____

_____

_____

2 _____

_____

_____

3 _____

_____

_____

4 _____

_____

_____

# Meditation

You asked the Holy Spirit to move. Now listen for God's voice. You can add music or keep it silent. Make a goal to add more time to this section over the coming weeks.

*Dream Life Every Day*

# Reflection

Did you sense God speaking to you? What do you believe He is calling you to do? Do you feel excited? Conflicted? Peaceful? Was anyone brought to your mind? Did you get a new idea? Now is the time to write it all down!

_____

_____

_____

_____

_____

_____

_____

_____

_____

_____

_____

_____

_____

_____

_____

_____

_____

_____

# Dream Life Goal

Writing your goal down each and every day creates momentum over time. Use this space to write down the Dream Life goal or other big goal you are working toward.

_____

_____

_____

_____

_____

_____

# Affirmations

Who will you be, how will you feel, and what will your life look like when your goal is complete? Write down the affirmations that correspond to the person you are becoming and the life you are creating. When you are done, read these affirmations out loud to yourself.

**I am** _____

**I am** _____

**I am** _____

**I am** _____

**I am** _____

# Visualization

Cement your big goal in your mind by picturing yourself achieving it. What will your life look like when your goal is completed? Notice any new details you can see today.

_Dream Life Every Day_

# Dream Life Goal Action Items:

Remember, this to-do list is not about laundry, groceries, or baths for the kids. These are action-oriented steps for today that will move you toward your goal. Make sure they are all small enough and specific enough to accomplish and check off your list today.

- ☐ _____
- ☐ _____
- ☐ _____
- ☐ _____
- ☐ _____

# Dream Health Action Item:

List one health-conscious thing you plan to do today. Is it to improve your water intake? Make more time for exercise? Tweak your menu or your sleep time?

- ☐ _____

# Dream Relationship Action Items:

What can you do today to be more intentional about important relationships? Text your spouse? Connect with a friend? Plan special times with each of your children?

- ☐ _____
- ☐ _____
- ☐ _____
- ☐ _____

# Day 12

Believe you can and you're halfway there.

Theodore Roosevelt

# Morning Prayer

Thank You, God, for Your amazing power and work within my life. I see all that You orchestrate in my life and am grateful for Your influence. I am grateful for the people, the opportunities, and the experiences that are placed on my path. I will take bold steps to live out Your purpose in my life today. I am accomplishing my dreams and have joy within my heart. Thank You for the explosion of goodness today as I live fully engaged, with my heart and my eyes wide open to You. I choose to see You work within my life today and every day.

# Eyes Wide Open

Take a few moments to consider how God has made His presence known in your life lately. What prayers has He answered for you? How have you experienced Him in your life or surroundings?

_____

_____

_____

_____

_____

_____

# Gratitude Game
## My Life Motto

What is one word that would describe your life in these areas: finances, family, friendships, business, health, hobbies, and giving back? (Choose a separate word for each category.) Then write down your favorite thing about each of those areas.

**Finances**

_____

_____

**Family**

_____

_____

_____

**Friendships**

_____

_____

**Business**

_____

_____

**Health**

_____

_____

_____

**Hobbies**

_____

_____

**Giving Back**

_____

_____

# Prayer Requests

This is a special place of hope, victory, and healing. It is your opportunity to ask the Holy Spirit to move in certain situations and relationships. Rather than filing your complaints, tell Him how you'd like these situations and relationships to look. Jot down four specific requests below, being careful to focus on asking Him for victory in these areas instead of simply listing grievances. Be sure to pay attention over time to how things change.

1 _____

_____

_____

2 _____

_____

_____

3 _____

_____

_____

4 _____

_____

_____

# Meditation

You asked the Holy Spirit to move. Now listen for God's voice. You can add music or keep it silent. Make a goal to add more time to this section over the coming weeks.

*Dream Life Every Day*

# Reflection

Did you sense God speaking to you? What do you believe He is calling you to do? Do you feel excited? Conflicted? Peaceful? Was anyone brought to your mind? Did you get a new idea? Now is the time to write it all down!

_____

_____

_____

_____

_____

_____

_____

_____

_____

_____

_____

_____

_____

_____

_____

_____

_____

_____

# Dream Life Goal

Writing your goal down each and every day creates momentum over time. Use this space to write down the Dream Life goal or other big goal you are working toward.

_____

_____

_____

_____

_____

# Affirmations

Who will you be, how will you feel, and what will your life look like when your goal is complete? Write down the affirmations that correspond to the person you are becoming and the life you are creating. When you are done, read these affirmations out loud to yourself.

**I am** _____

**I am** _____

**I am** _____

**I am** _____

**I am** _____

# Visualization

Cement your big goal in your mind by picturing yourself achieving it. What will your life look like when your goal is completed? Notice any new details you can see today.

# Dream Life Goal Action Items:

Remember, this to-do list is not about laundry, groceries, or baths for the kids. These are action-oriented steps for today that will move you toward your goal. Make sure they are all small enough and specific enough to accomplish and check off your list today.

☐ _____

☐ _____

☐ _____

☐ _____

☐ _____

# Dream Health Action Item:

List one health-conscious thing you plan to do today. Is it to improve your water intake? Make more time for exercise? Tweak your menu or your sleep time?

☐ _____

# Dream Relationship Action Items:

What can you do today to be more intentional about important relationships? Text your spouse? Connect with a friend? Plan special times with each of your children?

☐ _____

☐ _____

☐ _____

☐ _____

# Day 13

Your mind is a powerful thing. When you fill it with positive thoughts, your life will start to change.

Unknown

# Morning Prayer

Thank You, God, for Your amazing power and work within my life. I see all that You orchestrate in my life and am grateful for Your influence. I am grateful for the people, the opportunities, and the experiences that are placed on my path. I will take bold steps to live out Your purpose in my life today. I am accomplishing my dreams and have joy within my heart. Thank You for the explosion of goodness today as I live fully engaged, with my heart and my eyes wide open to You. I choose to see You work within my life today and every day.

# Eyes Wide Open

Take a few moments to consider how God has made His presence known in your life lately. What prayers has He answered for you? How have you experienced Him in your life or surroundings?

_____

_____

_____

_____

_____

_____

# Gratitude Game
## All Around

Take a look around your home and write about several things you are grateful for. What about them fills you with gratitude?

# Prayer Requests

This is a special place of hope, victory, and healing. It is your opportunity to ask the Holy Spirit to move in certain situations and relationships. Rather than filing your complaints, tell Him how you'd like these situations and relationships to look. Jot down four specific requests below, being careful to focus on asking Him for victory in these areas instead of simply listing grievances. Be sure to pay attention over time to how things change.

1 _____

_____

_____

2 _____

_____

_____

3 _____

_____

_____

4 _____

_____

_____

# Meditation

You asked the Holy Spirit to move. Now listen for God's voice. You can add music or keep it silent. Make a goal to add more time to this section over the coming weeks.

*Dream Life Every Day*

# Reflection

Did you sense God speaking to you? What do you believe He is calling you to do? Do you feel excited? Conflicted? Peaceful? Was anyone brought to your mind? Did you get a new idea? Now is the time to write it all down!

_____

_____

_____

_____

_____

_____

_____

_____

_____

_____

_____

_____

_____

_____

_____

_____

_____

_____

# Dream Life Goal

Writing your goal down each and every day creates momentum over time. Use this space to write down the Dream Life goal or other big goal you are working toward.

_____

_____

_____

_____

_____

# Affirmations

Who will you be, how will you feel, and what will your life look like when your goal is complete? Write down the affirmations that correspond to the person you are becoming and the life you are creating. When you are done, read these affirmations out loud to yourself.

**I am** _____

**I am** _____

**I am** _____

**I am** _____

**I am** _____

# Visualization

Cement your big goal in your mind by picturing yourself achieving it. What will your life look like when your goal is completed? Notice any new details you can see today.

*Dream Life Every Day*

# Dream Life Goal Action Items:

Remember, this to-do list is not about laundry, groceries, or baths for the kids. These are action-oriented steps for today that will move you toward your goal. Make sure they are all small enough and specific enough to accomplish and check off your list today.

☐ _____

☐ _____

☐ _____

☐ _____

☐ _____

# Dream Health Action Item:

List one health-conscious thing you plan to do today. Is it to improve your water intake? Make more time for exercise? Tweak your menu or your sleep time?

☐ _____

# Dream Relationship Action Items:

What can you do today to be more intentional about important relationships? Text your spouse? Connect with a friend? Plan special times with each of your children?

☐ _____

☐ _____

☐ _____

☐ _____

# Day 14

Whatever you hold in your mind on a consistent basis is exactly what you will experience in your life.

Tony Robbins

# Morning Prayer

Thank You, God, for Your amazing power and work within my life. I see all that You orchestrate in my life and am grateful for Your influence. I am grateful for the people, the opportunities, and the experiences that are placed on my path. I will take bold steps to live out Your purpose in my life today. I am accomplishing my dreams and have joy within my heart. Thank You for the explosion of goodness today as I live fully engaged, with my heart and my eyes wide open to You. I choose to see You work within my life today and every day.

# Eyes Wide Open

Take a few moments to consider how God has made His presence known in your life lately. What prayers has He answered for you? How have you experienced Him in your life or surroundings?

_____

_____

_____

_____

_____

_____

_____

# Gratitude Game

## Strength Bound

List ten personal qualities or skills you have and how they impact the world.

*Dream Life Every Day*

1 _____

_____

2 _____

_____

3 _____

_____

4 _____

_____

5 _____

_____

6 _____

_____

7 _____

_____

8 _____

_____

9 _____

_____

10 _____

# Prayer Requests

This is a special place of hope, victory, and healing. It is your opportunity to ask the Holy Spirit to move in certain situations and relationships. Rather than filing your complaints, tell Him how you'd like these situations and relationships to look. Jot down four specific requests below, being careful to focus on asking Him for victory in these areas instead of simply listing grievances. Be sure to pay attention over time to how things change.

1 _____

_____

_____

2 _____

_____

_____

3 _____

_____

_____

4 _____

_____

_____

# Meditation

You asked the Holy Spirit to move. Now listen for God's voice. You can add music or keep it silent. Make a goal to add more time to this section over the coming weeks.

*Dream Life Every Day*

# Reflection

Did you sense God speaking to you? What do you believe He is calling you to do? Do you feel excited? Conflicted? Peaceful? Was anyone brought to your mind? Did you get a new idea? Now is the time to write it all down!

_____

_____

_____

_____

_____

_____

_____

_____

_____

_____

_____

_____

_____

_____

_____

_____

_____

_____

_____

_____

# Dream Life Goal

Writing your goal down each and every day creates momentum over time. Use this space to write down the Dream Life goal or other big goal you are working toward.

_____

_____

_____

_____

_____

_____

# Affirmations

Who will you be, how will you feel, and what will your life look like when your goal is complete? Write down the affirmations that correspond to the person you are becoming and the life you are creating. When you are done, read these affirmations out loud to yourself.

**I am** _____

**I am** _____

**I am** _____

**I am** _____

**I am** _____

# Visualization

Cement your big goal in your mind by picturing yourself achieving it. What will your life look like when your goal is completed? Notice any new details you can see today.

# Dream Life Goal Action Items:

Remember, this to-do list is not about laundry, groceries, or baths for the kids. These are action-oriented steps for today that will move you toward your goal. Make sure they are all small enough and specific enough to accomplish and check off your list today.

- ☐ _____
- ☐ _____
- ☐ _____
- ☐ _____
- ☐ _____

# Dream Health Action Item:

List one health-conscious thing you plan to do today. Is it to improve your water intake? Make more time for exercise? Tweak your menu or your sleep time?

- ☐ _____

# Dream Relationship Action Items:

What can you do today to be more intentional about important relationships? Text your spouse? Connect with a friend? Plan special times with each of your children?

- ☐ _____
- ☐ _____
- ☐ _____
- ☐ _____

# Day 15

Most of the important things in the world have been accomplished by people who have kept on trying when there seemed to be no hope at all.

Dale Carnegie

# Morning Prayer

Thank You, God, for Your amazing power and work within my life. I see all that You orchestrate in my life and am grateful for Your influence. I am grateful for the people, the opportunities, and the experiences that are placed on my path. I will take bold steps to live out Your purpose in my life today. I am accomplishing my dreams and have joy within my heart. Thank You for the explosion of goodness today as I live fully engaged, with my heart and my eyes wide open to You. I choose to see You work within my life today and every day.

# Eyes Wide Open

Take a few moments to consider how God has made His presence known in your life lately. What prayers has He answered for you? How have you experienced Him in your life or surroundings?

_____

_____

_____

_____

_____

_____

# Gratitude Game
## Smile Big

Eyes up, shoulders back, and smile big! What attribute, quality, or physical characteristic are you most proud of, and why? How would it change your level of confidence if you imagined everyone seeing that trait first whenever they looked at you? Wherever you are today, think about what you like most about yourself, instead of what you don't, and then smile big to everyone you see.

_____

_____

_____

_____

_____

_____

_____

_____

_____

_____

_____

_____

_____

_____

_____

_____

_____

_____

_____

# Prayer Requests

This is a special place of hope, victory, and healing. It is your opportunity to ask the Holy Spirit to move in certain situations and relationships. Rather than filing your complaints, tell Him how you'd like these situations and relationships to look. Jot down four specific requests below, being careful to focus on asking Him for victory in these areas instead of simply listing grievances. Be sure to pay attention over time to how things change.

1 _____

_____

_____

2 _____

_____

_____

3 _____

_____

_____

4 _____

_____

_____

# Meditation

You asked the Holy Spirit to move. Now listen for God's voice. You can add music or keep it silent. Make a goal to add more time to this section over the coming weeks.

*Dream Life Every Day*

# Reflection

Did you sense God speaking to you? What do you believe He is calling you to do? Do you feel excited? Conflicted? Peaceful? Was anyone brought to your mind? Did you get a new idea? Now is the time to write it all down!

# Dream Life Goal

Writing your goal down each and every day creates momentum over time. Use this space to write down the Dream Life goal or other big goal you are working toward.

_____

_____

_____

_____

_____

# Affirmations

Who will you be, how will you feel, and what will your life look like when your goal is complete? Write down the affirmations that correspond to the person you are becoming and the life you are creating. When you are done, read these affirmations out loud to yourself.

**I am** _____

**I am** _____

**I am** _____

**I am** _____

**I am** _____

# Visualization

Cement your big goal in your mind by picturing yourself achieving it. What will your life look like when your goal is completed? Notice any new details you can see today.

# Dream Life Goal Action Items:

Remember, this to-do list is not about laundry, groceries, or baths for the kids. These are action-oriented steps for today that will move you toward your goal. Make sure they are all small enough and specific enough to accomplish and check off your list today.

- ☐ _____
- ☐ _____
- ☐ _____
- ☐ _____
- ☐ _____

# Dream Health Action Item:

List one health-conscious thing you plan to do today. Is it to improve your water intake? Make more time for exercise? Tweak your menu or your sleep time?

- ☐ _____

# Dream Relationship Action Items:

What can you do today to be more intentional about important relationships? Text your spouse? Connect with a friend? Plan special times with each of your children?

- ☐ _____
- ☐ _____
- ☐ _____
- ☐ _____

# Day 16

The future belongs to those who believe in the beauty of their dreams.
Eleanor Roosevelt

# Morning Prayer

Thank You, God, for Your amazing power and work within my life. I see all that You orchestrate in my life and am grateful for Your influence. I am grateful for the people, the opportunities, and the experiences that are placed on my path. I will take bold steps to live out Your purpose in my life today. I am accomplishing my dreams and have joy within my heart. Thank You for the explosion of goodness today as I live fully engaged, with my heart and my eyes wide open to You. I choose to see You work within my life today and every day.

# Eyes Wide Open

Take a few moments to consider how God has made His presence known in your life lately. What prayers has He answered for you? How have you experienced Him in your life or surroundings?

_____

_____

_____

_____

_____

_____

_____

# Gratitude Game

## Truly Alive

What makes you feel truly alive?

# Prayer Requests

This is a special place of hope, victory, and healing. It is your opportunity to ask the Holy Spirit to move in certain situations and relationships. Rather than filing your complaints, tell Him how you'd like these situations and relationships to look. Jot down four specific requests below, being careful to focus on asking Him for victory in these areas instead of simply listing grievances. Be sure to pay attention over time to how things change.

**1** _____

_____

_____

**2** _____

_____

_____

**3** _____

_____

_____

**4** _____

_____

_____

# Meditation

You asked the Holy Spirit to move. Now listen for God's voice. You can add music or keep it silent. Make a goal to add more time to this section over the coming weeks.

*Dream Life Every Day*

# Reflection

Did you sense God speaking to you? What do you believe He is calling you to do? Do you feel excited? Conflicted? Peaceful? Was anyone brought to your mind? Did you get a new idea? Now is the time to write it all down!

_____

_____

_____

_____

_____

_____

_____

_____

_____

_____

_____

_____

_____

_____

_____

_____

_____

_____

_____

# Dream Life Goal

Writing your goal down each and every day creates momentum over time. Use this space to write down the Dream Life goal or other big goal you are working toward.

_____

_____

_____

_____

_____

# Affirmations

Who will you be, how will you feel, and what will your life look like when your goal is complete? Write down the affirmations that correspond to the person you are becoming and the life you are creating. When you are done, read these affirmations out loud to yourself.

**I am** _____

**I am** _____

**I am** _____

**I am** _____

**I am** _____

# Visualization

Cement your big goal in your mind by picturing yourself achieving it. What will your life look like when your goal is completed? Notice any new details you can see today.

# Dream Life Goal Action Items:

Remember, this to-do list is not about laundry, groceries, or baths for the kids. These are action-oriented steps for today that will move you toward your goal. Make sure they are all small enough and specific enough to accomplish and check off your list today.

☐ _____

☐ _____

☐ _____

☐ _____

☐ _____

# Dream Health Action Item:

List one health-conscious thing you plan to do today. Is it to improve your water intake? Make more time for exercise? Tweak your menu or your sleep time?

☐ _____

# Dream Relationship Action Items:

What can you do today to be more intentional about important relationships? Text your spouse? Connect with a friend? Plan special times with each of your children?

☐ _____

☐ _____

☐ _____

☐ _____

# Day 17

If you can tune in to your purpose and really align with it, setting goals so that your vision is an expression of that purpose, then life flows much more easily.

Jack Canfield

# Morning Prayer

Thank You, God, for Your amazing power and work within my life. I see all that You orchestrate in my life and am grateful for Your influence. I am grateful for the people, the opportunities, and the experiences that are placed on my path. I will take bold steps to live out Your purpose in my life today. I am accomplishing my dreams and have joy within my heart. Thank You for the explosion of goodness today as I live fully engaged, with my heart and my eyes wide open to You. I choose to see You work within my life today and every day.

# Eyes Wide Open

Take a few moments to consider how God has made His presence known in your life lately. What prayers has He answered for you? How have you experienced Him in your life or surroundings?

_____

_____

_____

_____

_____

_____

# Gratitude Game
## Next Generation

What tradition(s) are you bringing from your younger years into your current home? What makes those traditions special? Which one most brings a smile to your face today?

# Prayer Requests

This is a special place of hope, victory, and healing. It is your opportunity to ask the Holy Spirit to move in certain situations and relationships. Rather than filing your complaints, tell Him how you'd like these situations and relationships to look. Jot down four specific requests below, being careful to focus on asking Him for victory in these areas instead of simply listing grievances. Be sure to pay attention over time to how things change.

**1** _____

_____

_____

**2** _____

_____

_____

**3** _____

_____

_____

**4** _____

_____

_____

# Meditation

You asked the Holy Spirit to move. Now listen for God's voice. You can add music or keep it silent. Make a goal to add more time to this section over the coming weeks.

# Reflection

Did you sense God speaking to you? What do you believe He is calling you to do? Do you feel excited? Conflicted? Peaceful? Was anyone brought to your mind? Did you get a new idea? Now is the time to write it all down!

# Dream Life Goal

Writing your goal down each and every day creates momentum over time. Use this space to write down the Dream Life goal or other big goal you are working toward.

_____

_____

_____

_____

_____

_____

# Affirmations

Who will you be, how will you feel, and what will your life look like when your goal is complete? Write down the affirmations that correspond to the person you are becoming and the life you are creating. When you are done, read these affirmations out loud to yourself.

**I am** _____

**I am** _____

**I am** _____

**I am** _____

**I am** _____

# Visualization

Cement your big goal in your mind by picturing yourself achieving it. What will your life look like when your goal is completed? Notice any new details you can see today.

# Dream Life Goal Action Items:

Remember, this to-do list is not about laundry, groceries, or baths for the kids. These are action-oriented steps for today that will move you toward your goal. Make sure they are all small enough and specific enough to accomplish and check off your list today.

- [ ] _____
- [ ] _____
- [ ] _____
- [ ] _____
- [ ] _____

# Dream Health Action Item:

List one health-conscious thing you plan to do today. Is it to improve your water intake? Make more time for exercise? Tweak your menu or your sleep time?

- [ ] _____

# Dream Relationship Action Items:

What can you do today to be more intentional about important relationships? Text your spouse? Connect with a friend? Plan special times with each of your children?

- [ ] _____
- [ ] _____
- [ ] _____
- [ ] _____

# Day 18

Whatever the mind can conceive and believe, it can achieve.

Napoleon Hill

# Morning Prayer

Thank You, God, for Your amazing power and work within my life. I see all that You orchestrate in my life and am grateful for Your influence. I am grateful for the people, the opportunities, and the experiences that are placed on my path. I will take bold steps to live out Your purpose in my life today. I am accomplishing my dreams and have joy within my heart. Thank You for the explosion of goodness today as I live fully engaged, with my heart and my eyes wide open to You. I choose to see You work within my life today and every day.

# Eyes Wide Open

Take a few moments to consider how God has made His presence known in your life lately. What prayers has He answered for you? How have you experienced Him in your life or surroundings?

_____

_____

_____

_____

_____

_____

# Gratitude Game
## Picture Time!

What's your favorite "normal" activity with your family or close friends? What makes it more special than the others?

Choose to cherish today as if it were a special occasion. Take pictures of your loved ones all day—at breakfast, dinner, school time, bedtime, or simply hanging out.

# Prayer Requests

This is a special place of hope, victory, and healing. It is your opportunity to ask the Holy Spirit to move in certain situations and relationships. Rather than filing your complaints, tell Him how you'd like these situations and relationships to look. Jot down four specific requests below, being careful to focus on asking Him for victory in these areas instead of simply listing grievances. Be sure to pay attention over time to how things change.

1 _____

_____

_____

2 _____

_____

_____

3 _____

_____

_____

4 _____

_____

_____

# Meditation

You asked the Holy Spirit to move. Now listen for God's voice. You can add music or keep it silent. Make a goal to add more time to this section over the coming weeks.

*Dream Life Every Day*

# Reflection

Did you sense God speaking to you? What do you believe He is calling you to do? Do you feel excited? Conflicted? Peaceful? Was anyone brought to your mind? Did you get a new idea? Now is the time to write it all down!

_____

_____

_____

_____

_____

_____

_____

_____

_____

_____

_____

_____

_____

_____

_____

_____

_____

_____

_____

_____

_____

# Dream Life Goal

Writing your goal down each and every day creates momentum over time. Use this space to write down the Dream Life goal or other big goal you are working toward.

_____

_____

_____

_____

_____

_____

# Affirmations

Who will you be, how will you feel, and what will your life look like when your goal is complete? Write down the affirmations that correspond to the person you are becoming and the life you are creating. When you are done, read these affirmations out loud to yourself.

**I am** _____

**I am** _____

**I am** _____

**I am** _____

**I am** _____

# Visualization

Cement your big goal in your mind by picturing yourself achieving it. What will your life look like when your goal is completed? Notice any new details you can see today.

# Dream Life Goal Action Items:

Remember, this to-do list is not about laundry, groceries, or baths for the kids. These are action-oriented steps for today that will move you toward your goal. Make sure they are all small enough and specific enough to accomplish and check off your list today.

- ☐ _____
- ☐ _____
- ☐ _____
- ☐ _____
- ☐ _____

# Dream Health Action Item:

List one health-conscious thing you plan to do today. Is it to improve your water intake? Make more time for exercise? Tweak your menu or your sleep time?

- ☐ _____

# Dream Relationship Action Items:

What can you do today to be more intentional about important relationships? Text your spouse? Connect with a friend? Plan special times with each of your children?

- ☐ _____
- ☐ _____
- ☐ _____
- ☐ _____

# Day 19

The quality of a person's life is in direct proportion to their commitment to excellence, regardless of their chosen field of endeavor.

Vince Lombardi

# Morning Prayer

Thank You, God, for Your amazing power and work within my life. I see all that You orchestrate in my life and am grateful for Your influence. I am grateful for the people, the opportunities, and the experiences that are placed on my path. I will take bold steps to live out Your purpose in my life today. I am accomplishing my dreams and have joy within my heart. Thank You for the explosion of goodness today as I live fully engaged, with my heart and my eyes wide open to You. I choose to see You work within my life today and every day.

# Eyes Wide Open

Take a few moments to consider how God has made His presence known in your life lately. What prayers has He answered for you? How have you experienced Him in your life or surroundings?

_____

_____

_____

_____

_____

_____

# Gratitude Game
## That's So Interesting

What are your interests and favorite hobbies? What about doing them brings you joy? Do you make enough time for them?

# Prayer Requests

This is a special place of hope, victory, and healing. It is your opportunity to ask the Holy Spirit to move in certain situations and relationships. Rather than filing your complaints, tell Him how you'd like these situations and relationships to look. Jot down four specific requests below, being careful to focus on asking Him for victory in these areas instead of simply listing grievances. Be sure to pay attention over time to how things change.

1 _____

_____

_____

2 _____

_____

_____

3 _____

_____

_____

4 _____

_____

_____

# Meditation

You asked the Holy Spirit to move. Now listen for God's voice. You can add music or keep it silent. Make a goal to add more time to this section over the coming weeks.

*Dream Life Every Day*

# Reflection

Did you sense God speaking to you? What do you believe He is calling you to do? Do you feel excited? Conflicted? Peaceful? Was anyone brought to your mind? Did you get a new idea? Now is the time to write it all down!

_____

_____

_____

_____

_____

_____

_____

_____

_____

_____

_____

_____

_____

_____

_____

_____

_____

_____

_____

# Dream Life Goal

Writing your goal down each and every day creates momentum over time. Use this space to write down the Dream Life goal or other big goal you are working toward.

_____

_____

_____

_____

_____

_____

# Affirmations

Who will you be, how will you feel, and what will your life look like when your goal is complete? Write down the affirmations that correspond to the person you are becoming and the life you are creating. When you are done, read these affirmations out loud to yourself.

**I am** _____

**I am** _____

**I am** _____

**I am** _____

**I am** _____

# Visualization

Cement your big goal in your mind by picturing yourself achieving it. What will your life look like when your goal is completed? Notice any new details you can see today.

_Dream Life Every Day_

# Dream Life Goal Action Items:

Remember, this to-do list is not about laundry, groceries, or baths for the kids. These are action-oriented steps for today that will move you toward your goal. Make sure they are all small enough and specific enough to accomplish and check off your list today.

☐ _____

☐ _____

☐ _____

☐ _____

☐ _____

# Dream Health Action Item:

List one health-conscious thing you plan to do today. Is it to improve your water intake? Make more time for exercise? Tweak your menu or your sleep time?

☐ _____

# Dream Relationship Action Items:

What can you do today to be more intentional about important relationships? Text your spouse? Connect with a friend? Plan special times with each of your children?

☐ _____

☐ _____

☐ _____

☐ _____

# Day 20

Do not be anxious about anything, but in every situation, by prayer and petition, with thanksgiving, present your requests to God. And the peace of God, which transcends all understanding, will guard your hearts and your minds in Christ Jesus.

Philippians 4:6–7

# Morning Prayer

Thank You, God, for Your amazing power and work within my life. I see all that You orchestrate in my life and am grateful for Your influence. I am grateful for the people, the opportunities, and the experiences that are placed on my path. I will take bold steps to live out Your purpose in my life today. I am accomplishing my dreams and have joy within my heart. Thank You for the explosion of goodness today as I live fully engaged, with my heart and my eyes wide open to You. I choose to see You work within my life today and every day.

# Eyes Wide Open

Take a few moments to consider how God has made His presence known in your life lately. What prayers has He answered for you? How have you experienced Him in your life or surroundings?

_____

_____

_____

_____

_____

_____

# Gratitude Game
## The Best Thing Since Sliced Bread

What is your favorite appliance, service, or amenity? How does it make your life easier, and what impact does that have on your attitude and emotional state? (For example, "I love my pressure cooker because I don't have to think about defrosting meat before dinner. I can be flexible and still prepare healthy meals for my family, which makes me happy and helps me stay in our family budget.")

# Prayer Requests

This is a special place of hope, victory, and healing. It is your opportunity to ask the Holy Spirit to move in certain situations and relationships. Rather than filing your complaints, tell Him how you'd like these situations and relationships to look. Jot down four specific requests below, being careful to focus on asking Him for victory in these areas instead of simply listing grievances. Be sure to pay attention over time to how things change.

1 _____

_____

_____

2 _____

_____

_____

3 _____

_____

_____

4 _____

_____

_____

# Meditation

You asked the Holy Spirit to move. Now listen for God's voice. You can add music or keep it silent. Make a goal to add more time to this section over the coming weeks.

*Dream Life Every Day*

# Reflection

Did you sense God speaking to you? What do you believe He is calling you to do? Do you feel excited? Conflicted? Peaceful? Was anyone brought to your mind? Did you get a new idea? Now is the time to write it all down!

_____

_____

_____

_____

_____

_____

_____

_____

_____

_____

_____

_____

_____

_____

_____

_____

# Dream Life Goal

Writing your goal down each and every day creates momentum over time. Use this space to write down the Dream Life goal or other big goal you are working toward.

_____

_____

_____

_____

_____

# Affirmations

Who will you be, how will you feel, and what will your life look like when your goal is complete? Write down the affirmations that correspond to the person you are becoming and the life you are creating. When you are done, read these affirmations out loud to yourself.

**I am** _____

**I am** _____

**I am** _____

**I am** _____

**I am** _____

# Visualization

Cement your big goal in your mind by picturing yourself achieving it. What will your life look like when your goal is completed? Notice any new details you can see today.

_Dream Life Every Day_

# Dream Life Goal Action Items:

Remember, this to-do list is not about laundry, groceries, or baths for the kids. These are action-oriented steps for today that will move you toward your goal. Make sure they are all small enough and specific enough to accomplish and check off your list today.

- [ ] _____
- [ ] _____
- [ ] _____
- [ ] _____
- [ ] _____

# Dream Health Action Item:

List one health-conscious thing you plan to do today. Is it to improve your water intake? Make more time for exercise? Tweak your menu or your sleep time?

- [ ] _____

# Dream Relationship Action Items:

What can you do today to be more intentional about important relationships? Text your spouse? Connect with a friend? Plan special times with each of your children?

- [ ] _____
- [ ] _____
- [ ] _____
- [ ] _____

# Day 21

It's not about perfect. It's about effort. And when you bring that effort every single day, that's where transformation happens. That's how change occurs.

Jillian Michaels

# Morning Prayer

Thank You, God, for Your amazing power and work within my life. I see all that You orchestrate in my life and am grateful for Your influence. I am grateful for the people, the opportunities, and the experiences that are placed on my path. I will take bold steps to live out Your purpose in my life today. I am accomplishing my dreams and have joy within my heart. Thank You for the explosion of goodness today as I live fully engaged, with my heart and my eyes wide open to You. I choose to see You work within my life today and every day.

# Eyes Wide Open

Take a few moments to consider how God has made His presence known in your life lately. What prayers has He answered for you? How have you experienced Him in your life or surroundings?

_____

_____

_____

_____

_____

_____

# Gratitude Game
## The Power of Music

Music often has the ability to lift our spirits, even during a down day. What song lifts your spirits and brings you joy, and why?

# Prayer Requests

This is a special place of hope, victory, and healing. It is your opportunity to ask the Holy Spirit to move in certain situations and relationships. Rather than filing your complaints, tell Him how you'd like these situations and relationships to look. Jot down four specific requests below, being careful to focus on asking Him for victory in these areas instead of simply listing grievances. Be sure to pay attention over time to how things change.

1 _____

_____

_____

2 _____

_____

_____

3 _____

_____

_____

4 _____

_____

_____

# Meditation

You asked the Holy Spirit to move. Now listen for God's voice. You can add music or keep it silent. Make a goal to add more time to this section over the coming weeks.

*Dream Life Every Day*

# Reflection

Did you sense God speaking to you? What do you believe He is calling you to do? Do you feel excited? Conflicted? Peaceful? Was anyone brought to your mind? Did you get a new idea? Now is the time to write it all down!

_____

_____

_____

_____

_____

_____

_____

_____

_____

_____

_____

_____

_____

_____

_____

_____

_____

_____

_____

_____

# Dream Life Goal

Writing your goal down each and every day creates momentum over time. Use this space to write down the Dream Life goal or other big goal you are working toward.

_____

_____

_____

_____

_____

_____

# Affirmations

Who will you be, how will you feel, and what will your life look like when your goal is complete? Write down the affirmations that correspond to the person you are becoming and the life you are creating. When you are done, read these affirmations out loud to yourself.

**I am** _____

**I am** _____

**I am** _____

**I am** _____

**I am** _____

# Visualization

Cement your big goal in your mind by picturing yourself achieving it. What will your life look like when your goal is completed? Notice any new details you can see today.

_Dream Life Every Day_

# Dream Life Goal Action Items:

Remember, this to-do list is not about laundry, groceries, or baths for the kids. These are action-oriented steps for today that will move you toward your goal. Make sure they are all small enough and specific enough to accomplish and check off your list today.

- [ ] _____
- [ ] _____
- [ ] _____
- [ ] _____
- [ ] _____

# Dream Health Action Item:

List one health-conscious thing you plan to do today. Is it to improve your water intake? Make more time for exercise? Tweak your menu or your sleep time?

- [ ] _____

# Dream Relationship Action Items:

What can you do today to be more intentional about important relationships? Text your spouse? Connect with a friend? Plan special times with each of your children?

- [ ] _____
- [ ] _____
- [ ] _____
- [ ] _____

# Day 22

Go confidently in the direction of your dreams. Live the life you've imagined.

Henry David Thoreau

# Morning Prayer

Thank You, God, for Your amazing power and work within my life. I see all that You orchestrate in my life and am grateful for Your influence. I am grateful for the people, the opportunities, and the experiences that are placed on my path. I will take bold steps to live out Your purpose in my life today. I am accomplishing my dreams and have joy within my heart. Thank You for the explosion of goodness today as I live fully engaged, with my heart and my eyes wide open to You. I choose to see You work within my life today and every day.

# Eyes Wide Open

Take a few moments to consider how God has made His presence known in your life lately. What prayers has He answered for you? How have you experienced Him in your life or surroundings?

_____

_____

_____

_____

_____

_____

# Gratitude Game
## Vacation Day

Think about your daily to-do list. What are the non-negotiables for you every day? Write them down, along with an explanation of how doing them adds value to your life.

*Dream Life Every Day*

# Prayer Requests

This is a special place of hope, victory, and healing. It is your opportunity to ask the Holy Spirit to move in certain situations and relationships. Rather than filing your complaints, tell Him how you'd like these situations and relationships to look. Jot down four specific requests below, being careful to focus on asking Him for victory in these areas instead of simply listing grievances. Be sure to pay attention over time to how things change.

1 _____

_____

_____

2 _____

_____

_____

3 _____

_____

_____

4 _____

_____

_____

# Meditation

You asked the Holy Spirit to move. Now listen for God's voice. You can add music or keep it silent. Make a goal to add more time to this section over the coming weeks.

*Dream Life Every Day*

# Reflection

Did you sense God speaking to you? What do you believe He is calling you to do? Do you feel excited? Conflicted? Peaceful? Was anyone brought to your mind? Did you get a new idea? Now is the time to write it all down!

_____

_____

_____

_____

_____

_____

_____

_____

_____

_____

_____

_____

_____

_____

_____

_____

_____

_____

_____

_____

# Dream Life Goal

Writing your goal down each and every day creates momentum over time. Use this space to write down the Dream Life goal or other big goal you are working toward.

_____

_____

_____

_____

_____

# Affirmations

Who will you be, how will you feel, and what will your life look like when your goal is complete? Write down the affirmations that correspond to the person you are becoming and the life you are creating. When you are done, read these affirmations out loud to yourself.

**I am** _____

**I am** _____

**I am** _____

**I am** _____

**I am** _____

# Visualization

Cement your big goal in your mind by picturing yourself achieving it. What will your life look like when your goal is completed? Notice any new details you can see today.

_Dream Life Every Day_

# Dream Life Goal Action Items:

Remember, this to-do list is not about laundry, groceries, or baths for the kids. These are action-oriented steps for today that will move you toward your goal. Make sure they are all small enough and specific enough to accomplish and check off your list today.

- ☐ _____
- ☐ _____
- ☐ _____
- ☐ _____
- ☐ _____

# Dream Health Action Item:

List one health-conscious thing you plan to do today. Is it to improve your water intake? Make more time for exercise? Tweak your menu or your sleep time?

- ☐ _____

# Dream Relationship Action Items:

What can you do today to be more intentional about important relationships? Text your spouse? Connect with a friend? Plan special times with each of your children?

- ☐ _____
- ☐ _____
- ☐ _____
- ☐ _____

# Day 23

You will get all you want in life if you help enough other people get what they want.

Zig Ziglar

# Morning Prayer

Thank You, God, for Your amazing power and work within my life. I see all that You orchestrate in my life and am grateful for Your influence. I am grateful for the people, the opportunities, and the experiences that are placed on my path. I will take bold steps to live out Your purpose in my life today. I am accomplishing my dreams and have joy within my heart. Thank You for the explosion of goodness today as I live fully engaged, with my heart and my eyes wide open to You. I choose to see You work within my life today and every day.

# Eyes Wide Open

Take a few moments to consider how God has made His presence known in your life lately. What prayers has He answered for you? How have you experienced Him in your life or surroundings?

_____

_____

_____

_____

_____

_____

# Gratitude Game

## Spread the Love

Think of five people you love. Why are they so special to you? Use your response to write notes to each of those people. Deliver them in the next couple of days.

# Prayer Requests

This is a special place of hope, victory, and healing. It is your opportunity to ask the Holy Spirit to move in certain situations and relationships. Rather than filing your complaints, tell Him how you'd like these situations and relationships to look. Jot down four specific requests below, being careful to focus on asking Him for victory in these areas instead of simply listing grievances. Be sure to pay attention over time to how things change.

1 _____

_____

_____

2 _____

_____

_____

3 _____

_____

_____

4 _____

_____

_____

# Meditation

You asked the Holy Spirit to move. Now listen for God's voice. You can add music or keep it silent. Make a goal to add more time to this section over the coming weeks.

*Dream Life Every Day*

# Reflection

Did you sense God speaking to you? What do you believe He is calling you to do? Do you feel excited? Conflicted? Peaceful? Was anyone brought to your mind? Did you get a new idea? Now is the time to write it all down!

_____

_____

_____

_____

_____

_____

_____

_____

_____

_____

_____

_____

_____

_____

_____

_____

_____

_____

# Dream Life Goal

Writing your goal down each and every day creates momentum over time. Use this space to write down the Dream Life goal or other big goal you are working toward.

_____

_____

_____

_____

_____

# Affirmations

Who will you be, how will you feel, and what will your life look like when your goal is complete? Write down the affirmations that correspond to the person you are becoming and the life you are creating. When you are done, read these affirmations out loud to yourself.

**I am** _____

**I am** _____

**I am** _____

**I am** _____

**I am** _____

# Visualization

Cement your big goal in your mind by picturing yourself achieving it. What will your life look like when your goal is completed? Notice any new details you can see today.

_Dream Life Every Day_

# Dream Life Goal Action Items:

Remember, this to-do list is not about laundry, groceries, or baths for the kids. These are action-oriented steps for today that will move you toward your goal. Make sure they are all small enough and specific enough to accomplish and check off your list today.

☐ _____

☐ _____

☐ _____

☐ _____

☐ _____

# Dream Health Action Item:

List one health-conscious thing you plan to do today. Is it to improve your water intake? Make more time for exercise? Tweak your menu or your sleep time?

☐ _____

# Dream Relationship Action Items:

What can you do today to be more intentional about important relationships? Text your spouse? Connect with a friend? Plan special times with each of your children?

☐ _____

☐ _____

☐ _____

☐ _____

# Day 24

I am convinced that life is 10 percent what happens to me and 90 percent how I react to it.

Charles R. Swindoll

# Morning Prayer

Thank You, God, for Your amazing power and work within my life. I see all that You orchestrate in my life and am grateful for Your influence. I am grateful for the people, the opportunities, and the experiences that are placed on my path. I will take bold steps to live out Your purpose in my life today. I am accomplishing my dreams and have joy within my heart. Thank You for the explosion of goodness today as I live fully engaged, with my heart and my eyes wide open to You. I choose to see You work within my life today and every day.

# Eyes Wide Open

Take a few moments to consider how God has made His presence known in your life lately. What prayers has He answered for you? How have you experienced Him in your life or surroundings?

_____

_____

_____

_____

_____

_____

_____

# Gratitude Game

## This Is Home

Describe what the feeling of _home_ means to you.

# Prayer Requests

This is a special place of hope, victory, and healing. It is your opportunity to ask the Holy Spirit to move in certain situations and relationships. Rather than filing your complaints, tell Him how you'd like these situations and relationships to look. Jot down four specific requests below, being careful to focus on asking Him for victory in these areas instead of simply listing grievances. Be sure to pay attention over time to how things change.

1 _____

_____

_____

2 _____

_____

_____

3 _____

_____

_____

4 _____

_____

_____

# Meditation

You asked the Holy Spirit to move. Now listen for God's voice. You can add music or keep it silent. Make a goal to add more time to this section over the coming weeks.

# Reflection

Did you sense God speaking to you? What do you believe He is calling you to do? Do you feel excited? Conflicted? Peaceful? Was anyone brought to your mind? Did you get a new idea? Now is the time to write it all down!

# Dream Life Goal

Writing your goal down each and every day creates momentum over time. Use this space to write down the Dream Life goal or other big goal you are working toward.

_____

_____

_____

_____

_____

# Affirmations

Who will you be, how will you feel, and what will your life look like when your goal is complete? Write down the affirmations that correspond to the person you are becoming and the life you are creating. When you are done, read these affirmations out loud to yourself.

**I am** _____

**I am** _____

**I am** _____

**I am** _____

**I am** _____

# Visualization

Cement your big goal in your mind by picturing yourself achieving it. What will your life look like when your goal is completed? Notice any new details you can see today.

# Dream Life Goal Action Items:

Remember, this to-do list is not about laundry, groceries, or baths for the kids. These are action-oriented steps for today that will move you toward your goal. Make sure they are all small enough and specific enough to accomplish and check off your list today.

- [ ] _____
- [ ] _____
- [ ] _____
- [ ] _____
- [ ] _____

# Dream Health Action Item:

List one health-conscious thing you plan to do today. Is it to improve your water intake? Make more time for exercise? Tweak your menu or your sleep time?

- [ ] _____

# Dream Relationship Action Items:

What can you do today to be more intentional about important relationships? Text your spouse? Connect with a friend? Plan special times with each of your children?

- [ ] _____
- [ ] _____
- [ ] _____
- [ ] _____

# Day 25

Look at the birds. They don't plant or harvest or store food in barns, for your heavenly Father feeds them. And aren't you far more valuable to him than they are?

Matthew 6:26, NLT

# Morning Prayer

Thank You, God, for Your amazing power and work within my life. I see all that You orchestrate in my life and am grateful for Your influence. I am grateful for the people, the opportunities, and the experiences that are placed on my path. I will take bold steps to live out Your purpose in my life today. I am accomplishing my dreams and have joy within my heart. Thank You for the explosion of goodness today as I live fully engaged, with my heart and my eyes wide open to You. I choose to see You work within my life today and every day.

# Eyes Wide Open

Take a few moments to consider how God has made His presence known in your life lately. What prayers has He answered for you? How have you experienced Him in your life or surroundings?

_____

_____

_____

_____

_____

_____

_____

# Gratitude Game

## Everyday Staycation

What is the best thing about being in your home? What do you most like to do when you're there?

# Prayer Requests

This is a special place of hope, victory, and healing. It is your opportunity to ask the Holy Spirit to move in certain situations and relationships. Rather than filing your complaints, tell Him how you'd like these situations and relationships to look. Jot down four specific requests below, being careful to focus on asking Him for victory in these areas instead of simply listing grievances. Be sure to pay attention over time to how things change.

1 _____

_____

_____

2 _____

_____

_____

3 _____

_____

_____

4 _____

_____

_____

# Meditation

You asked the Holy Spirit to move. Now listen for God's voice. You can add music or keep it silent. Make a goal to add more time to this section over the coming weeks.

# Reflection

Did you sense God speaking to you? What do you believe He is calling you to do? Do you feel excited? Conflicted? Peaceful? Was anyone brought to your mind? Did you get a new idea? Now is the time to write it all down!

# Dream Life Goal

Writing your goal down each and every day creates momentum over time. Use this space to write down the Dream Life goal or other big goal you are working toward.

_____

_____

_____

_____

_____

_____

# Affirmations

Who will you be, how will you feel, and what will your life look like when your goal is complete? Write down the affirmations that correspond to the person you are becoming and the life you are creating. When you are done, read these affirmations out loud to yourself.

**I am** _____

**I am** _____

**I am** _____

**I am** _____

**I am** _____

# Visualization

Cement your big goal in your mind by picturing yourself achieving it. What will your life look like when your goal is completed? Notice any new details you can see today.

_Dream Life Every Day_

# Dream Life Goal Action Items:

Remember, this to-do list is not about laundry, groceries, or baths for the kids. These are action-oriented steps for today that will move you toward your goal. Make sure they are all small enough and specific enough to accomplish and check off your list today.

- ☐ _____
- ☐ _____
- ☐ _____
- ☐ _____
- ☐ _____

# Dream Health Action Item:

List one health-conscious thing you plan to do today. Is it to improve your water intake? Make more time for exercise? Tweak your menu or your sleep time?

- ☐ _____

# Dream Relationship Action Items:

What can you do today to be more intentional about important relationships? Text your spouse? Connect with a friend? Plan special times with each of your children?

- ☐ _____
- ☐ _____
- ☐ _____
- ☐ _____

# Day 26

Inaction breeds doubt and fear. Action breeds confidence and courage. If you want to conquer fear, do not sit home and think about it. Go out and get busy.

Dale Carnegie

# Morning Prayer

Thank You, God, for Your amazing power and work within my life. I see all that You orchestrate in my life and am grateful for Your influence. I am grateful for the people, the opportunities, and the experiences that are placed on my path. I will take bold steps to live out Your purpose in my life today. I am accomplishing my dreams and have joy within my heart. Thank You for the explosion of goodness today as I live fully engaged, with my heart and my eyes wide open to You. I choose to see You work within my life today and every day.

# Eyes Wide Open

Take a few moments to consider how God has made His presence known in your life lately. What prayers has He answered for you? How have you experienced Him in your life or surroundings?

_____

_____

_____

_____

_____

_____

# Gratitude Game
## Say Cheese

Take a moment to scroll through the camera roll on your phone or look at any printed photos around you. Which brings you the most joy, and why?

# Prayer Requests

This is a special place of hope, victory, and healing. It is your opportunity to ask the Holy Spirit to move in certain situations and relationships. Rather than filing your complaints, tell Him how you'd like these situations and relationships to look. Jot down four specific requests below, being careful to focus on asking Him for victory in these areas instead of simply listing grievances. Be sure to pay attention over time to how things change.

**1** _____

_____

_____

**2** _____

_____

_____

**3** _____

_____

_____

**4** _____

_____

_____

# Meditation

You asked the Holy Spirit to move. Now listen for God's voice. You can add music or keep it silent. Make a goal to add more time to this section over the coming weeks.

# Reflection

Did you sense God speaking to you? What do you believe He is calling you to do? Do you feel excited? Conflicted? Peaceful? Was anyone brought to your mind? Did you get a new idea? Now is the time to write it all down!

_____

_____

_____

_____

_____

_____

_____

_____

_____

_____

_____

_____

_____

_____

_____

_____

_____

_____

# Dream Life Goal

Writing your goal down each and every day creates momentum over time. Use this space to write down the Dream Life goal or other big goal you are working toward.

_____

_____

_____

_____

_____

# Affirmations

Who will you be, how will you feel, and what will your life look like when your goal is complete? Write down the affirmations that correspond to the person you are becoming and the life you are creating. When you are done, read these affirmations out loud to yourself.

**I am** _____

**I am** _____

**I am** _____

**I am** _____

**I am** _____

# Visualization

Cement your big goal in your mind by picturing yourself achieving it. What will your life look like when your goal is completed? Notice any new details you can see today.

_Dream Life Every Day_

# Dream Life Goal Action Items:

Remember, this to-do list is not about laundry, groceries, or baths for the kids. These are action-oriented steps for today that will move you toward your goal. Make sure they are all small enough and specific enough to accomplish and check off your list today.

- [ ] _____
- [ ] _____
- [ ] _____
- [ ] _____
- [ ] _____

# Dream Health Action Item:

List one health-conscious thing you plan to do today. Is it to improve your water intake? Make more time for exercise? Tweak your menu or your sleep time?

- [ ] _____

# Dream Relationship Action Items:

What can you do today to be more intentional about important relationships? Text your spouse? Connect with a friend? Plan special times with each of your children?

- [ ] _____
- [ ] _____
- [ ] _____
- [ ] _____

# Day 27

If you don't design your own life plan, chances are you'll fall into someone else's plan. And guess what they have planned for you? Not much.

Jim Rohn

# Morning Prayer

Thank You, God, for Your amazing power and work within my life. I see all that You orchestrate in my life and am grateful for Your influence. I am grateful for the people, the opportunities, and the experiences that are placed on my path. I will take bold steps to live out Your purpose in my life today. I am accomplishing my dreams and have joy within my heart. Thank You for the explosion of goodness today as I live fully engaged, with my heart and my eyes wide open to You. I choose to see You work within my life today and every day.

# Eyes Wide Open

Take a few moments to consider how God has made His presence known in your life lately. What prayers has He answered for you? How have you experienced Him in your life or surroundings?

_____

_____

_____

_____

_____

_____

_____

# Gratitude Game

## Ripple Effect

Who inspires you the most? Why does he or she inspire you?

# Prayer Requests

This is a special place of hope, victory, and healing. It is your opportunity to ask the Holy Spirit to move in certain situations and relationships. Rather than filing your complaints, tell Him how you'd like these situations and relationships to look. Jot down four specific requests below, being careful to focus on asking Him for victory in these areas instead of simply listing grievances. Be sure to pay attention over time to how things change.

1 _____

_____

_____

2 _____

_____

_____

3 _____

_____

_____

4 _____

_____

_____

# Meditation

You asked the Holy Spirit to move. Now listen for God's voice. You can add music or keep it silent. Make a goal to add more time to this section over the coming weeks.

*Dream Life Every Day*

# Reflection

Did you sense God speaking to you? What do you believe He is calling you to do? Do you feel excited? Conflicted? Peaceful? Was anyone brought to your mind? Did you get a new idea? Now is the time to write it all down!

_____

_____

_____

_____

_____

_____

_____

_____

_____

_____

_____

_____

_____

_____

_____

_____

_____

_____

_____

# Dream Life Goal

Writing your goal down each and every day creates momentum over time. Use this space to write down the Dream Life goal or other big goal you are working toward.

_____

_____

_____

_____

_____

_____

# Affirmations

Who will you be, how will you feel, and what will your life look like when your goal is complete? Write down the affirmations that correspond to the person you are becoming and the life you are creating. When you are done, read these affirmations out loud to yourself.

**I am** _____

**I am** _____

**I am** _____

**I am** _____

**I am** _____

# Visualization

Cement your big goal in your mind by picturing yourself achieving it. What will your life look like when your goal is completed? Notice any new details you can see today.

*Dream Life Every Day*

# Dream Life Goal Action Items:

Remember, this to-do list is not about laundry, groceries, or baths for the kids. These are action-oriented steps for today that will move you toward your goal. Make sure they are all small enough and specific enough to accomplish and check off your list today.

- ☐ _____
- ☐ _____
- ☐ _____
- ☐ _____
- ☐ _____

# Dream Health Action Item:

List one health-conscious thing you plan to do today. Is it to improve your water intake? Make more time for exercise? Tweak your menu or your sleep time?

- ☐ _____

# Dream Relationship Action Items:

What can you do today to be more intentional about important relationships? Text your spouse? Connect with a friend? Plan special times with each of your children?

- ☐ _____
- ☐ _____
- ☐ _____
- ☐ _____

# Day 28

You control your future, your destiny. What you think about comes about. By recording your dreams and goals on paper, you set in motion the process of becoming the person you most want to be. Put your future in good hands—your own.

Mark Victor Hansen

# Morning Prayer

Thank You, God, for Your amazing power and work within my life. I see all that You orchestrate in my life and am grateful for Your influence. I am grateful for the people, the opportunities, and the experiences that are placed on my path. I will take bold steps to live out Your purpose in my life today. I am accomplishing my dreams and have joy within my heart. Thank You for the explosion of goodness today as I live fully engaged, with my heart and my eyes wide open to You. I choose to see You work within my life today and every day.

# Eyes Wide Open

Take a few moments to consider how God has made His presence known in your life lately. What prayers has He answered for you? How have you experienced Him in your life or surroundings?

_____

_____

_____

_____

_____

_____

# Gratitude Game
## A Friend Worth Celebrating

Imagine you were just given some incredible news. Who is the first person you'll call to celebrate with and why? How does his or her friendship make your life better?

_Dream Life Every Day_

# Prayer Requests

This is a special place of hope, victory, and healing. It is your opportunity to ask the Holy Spirit to move in certain situations and relationships. Rather than filing your complaints, tell Him how you'd like these situations and relationships to look. Jot down four specific requests below, being careful to focus on asking Him for victory in these areas instead of simply listing grievances. Be sure to pay attention over time to how things change.

1 _____

_____

_____

2 _____

_____

_____

3 _____

_____

_____

4 _____

_____

_____

# Meditation

You asked the Holy Spirit to move. Now listen for God's voice. You can add music or keep it silent. Make a goal to add more time to this section over the coming weeks.

*Dream Life Every Day*

# Reflection

Did you sense God speaking to you? What do you believe He is calling you to do? Do you feel excited? Conflicted? Peaceful? Was anyone brought to your mind? Did you get a new idea? Now is the time to write it all down!

_____

_____

_____

_____

_____

_____

_____

_____

_____

_____

_____

_____

_____

_____

_____

_____

_____

_____

_____

# Dream Life Goal

Writing your goal down each and every day creates momentum over time. Use this space to write down the Dream Life goal or other big goal you are working toward.

_____

_____

_____

_____

_____

# Affirmations

Who will you be, how will you feel, and what will your life look like when your goal is complete? Write down the affirmations that correspond to the person you are becoming and the life you are creating. When you are done, read these affirmations out loud to yourself.

**I am** _____

**I am** _____

**I am** _____

**I am** _____

**I am** _____

# Visualization

Cement your big goal in your mind by picturing yourself achieving it. What will your life look like when your goal is completed? Notice any new details you can see today.

_Dream Life Every Day_

# Dream Life Goal Action Items:

Remember, this to-do list is not about laundry, groceries, or baths for the kids. These are action-oriented steps for today that will move you toward your goal. Make sure they are all small enough and specific enough to accomplish and check off your list today.

- [ ] _____
- [ ] _____
- [ ] _____
- [ ] _____
- [ ] _____

# Dream Health Action Item:

List one health-conscious thing you plan to do today. Is it to improve your water intake? Make more time for exercise? Tweak your menu or your sleep time?

- [ ] _____

# Dream Relationship Action Items:

What can you do today to be more intentional about important relationships? Text your spouse? Connect with a friend? Plan special times with each of your children?

- [ ] _____
- [ ] _____
- [ ] _____
- [ ] _____

# Day 29

Make yourself so happy that when others look at you they become happy too.

Yogi Bhajan

# Morning Prayer

Thank You, God, for Your amazing power and work within my life. I see all that You orchestrate in my life and am grateful for Your influence. I am grateful for the people, the opportunities, and the experiences that are placed on my path. I will take bold steps to live out Your purpose in my life today. I am accomplishing my dreams and have joy within my heart. Thank You for the explosion of goodness today as I live fully engaged, with my heart and my eyes wide open to You. I choose to see You work within my life today and every day.

# Eyes Wide Open

Take a few moments to consider how God has made His presence known in your life lately. What prayers has He answered for you? How have you experienced Him in your life or surroundings?

_____

_____

_____

_____

_____

_____

# Gratitude Game

## Relationship Love

Think about your relationship with your spouse, children, or another close family member or friend. How has your relationship with them changed for the better in the last five years?

# Prayer Requests

This is a special place of hope, victory, and healing. It is your opportunity to ask the Holy Spirit to move in certain situations and relationships. Rather than filing your complaints, tell Him how you'd like these situations and relationships to look. Jot down four specific requests below, being careful to focus on asking Him for victory in these areas instead of simply listing grievances. Be sure to pay attention over time to how things change.

1 _____

_____

_____

2 _____

_____

_____

3 _____

_____

_____

4 _____

_____

_____

# Meditation

You asked the Holy Spirit to move. Now listen for God's voice. You can add music or keep it silent. Make a goal to add more time to this section over the coming weeks.

# Reflection

Did you sense God speaking to you? What do you believe He is calling you to do? Do you feel excited? Conflicted? Peaceful? Was anyone brought to your mind? Did you get a new idea? Now is the time to write it all down!

_____

_____

_____

_____

_____

_____

_____

_____

_____

_____

_____

_____

_____

_____

_____

_____

_____

_____

_____

# Dream Life Goal

Writing your goal down each and every day creates momentum over time. Use this space to write down the Dream Life goal or other big goal you are working toward.

_____

_____

_____

_____

_____

# Affirmations

Who will you be, how will you feel, and what will your life look like when your goal is complete? Write down the affirmations that correspond to the person you are becoming and the life you are creating. When you are done, read these affirmations out loud to yourself.

**I am** _____

**I am** _____

**I am** _____

**I am** _____

**I am** _____

# Visualization

Cement your big goal in your mind by picturing yourself achieving it. What will your life look like when your goal is completed? Notice any new details you can see today.

# Dream Life Goal Action Items:

Remember, this to-do list is not about laundry, groceries, or baths for the kids. These are action-oriented steps for today that will move you toward your goal. Make sure they are all small enough and specific enough to accomplish and check off your list today.

- ☐ _____
- ☐ _____
- ☐ _____
- ☐ _____
- ☐ _____

# Dream Health Action Item:

List one health-conscious thing you plan to do today. Is it to improve your water intake? Make more time for exercise? Tweak your menu or your sleep time?

- ☐ _____

# Dream Relationship Action Items:

What can you do today to be more intentional about important relationships? Text your spouse? Connect with a friend? Plan special times with each of your children?

- ☐ _____
- ☐ _____
- ☐ _____
- ☐ _____

# Day 30

Do everything in love.

1 Corinthians 16:14

# Morning Prayer

Thank You, God, for Your amazing power and work within my life. I see all that You orchestrate in my life and am grateful for Your influence. I am grateful for the people, the opportunities, and the experiences that are placed on my path. I will take bold steps to live out Your purpose in my life today. I am accomplishing my dreams and have joy within my heart. Thank You for the explosion of goodness today as I live fully engaged, with my heart and my eyes wide open to You. I choose to see You work within my life today and every day.

# Eyes Wide Open

Take a few moments to consider how God has made His presence known in your life lately. What prayers has He answered for you? How have you experienced Him in your life or surroundings?

_____

_____

_____

_____

_____

_____

# Gratitude Game
## Legacy

If there is one message you could leave the world, what is it? Why is it so important? How is your life proclaiming that message right now?

# Prayer Requests

This is a special place of hope, victory, and healing. It is your opportunity to ask the Holy Spirit to move in certain situations and relationships. Rather than filing your complaints, tell Him how you'd like these situations and relationships to look. Jot down four specific requests below, being careful to focus on asking Him for victory in these areas instead of simply listing grievances. Be sure to pay attention over time to how things change.

1 _____

_____

_____

2 _____

_____

_____

3 _____

_____

_____

4 _____

_____

_____

# Meditation

You asked the Holy Spirit to move. Now listen for God's voice. You can add music or keep it silent. Make a goal to add more time to this section over the coming weeks.

*Dream Life Every Day*

# Reflection

Did you sense God speaking to you? What do you believe He is calling you to do? Do you feel excited? Conflicted? Peaceful? Was anyone brought to your mind? Did you get a new idea? Now is the time to write it all down!

# Dream Life Goal

Writing your goal down each and every day creates momentum over time. Use this space to write down the Dream Life goal or other big goal you are working toward.

_____

_____

_____

_____

_____

_____

# Affirmations

Who will you be, how will you feel, and what will your life look like when your goal is complete? Write down the affirmations that correspond to the person you are becoming and the life you are creating. When you are done, read these affirmations out loud to yourself.

**I am** _____

**I am** _____

**I am** _____

**I am** _____

**I am** _____

# Visualization

Cement your big goal in your mind by picturing yourself achieving it. What will your life look like when your goal is completed? Notice any new details you can see today.

# Dream Life Goal Action Items:

Remember, this to-do list is not about laundry, groceries, or baths for the kids. These are action-oriented steps for today that will move you toward your goal. Make sure they are all small enough and specific enough to accomplish and check off your list today.

- ☐ _____
- ☐ _____
- ☐ _____
- ☐ _____
- ☐ _____

# Dream Health Action Item:

List one health-conscious thing you plan to do today. Is it to improve your water intake? Make more time for exercise? Tweak your menu or your sleep time?

- ☐ _____

# Dream Relationship Action Items:

What can you do today to be more intentional about important relationships? Text your spouse? Connect with a friend? Plan special times with each of your children?

- ☐ _____
- ☐ _____
- ☐ _____
- ☐ _____

> The best day of your life is the one on which you decide your life is your own. No apologies or excuses. No one to lean on, rely on, or blame. The gift is yours—it is an amazing journey—and you alone are responsible for the quality of it. This is the day your life really begins.
>
> Bob Moawad

# Conclusion

Congratulations! You are thirty days closer to living your Dream Life!

During the last month we have spent together, you have made and cemented habits that will change your life forever. Keep this going. These new habits are sending you down a new path—a path that leads toward success. Don't stop now. Continue connecting with your Dream Life goal daily and taking time each morning to determine a plan of action and execute it. Pick up another one of the journals in the Dream Life series and go through it, or do this one again. Remember, what the mind sees, the body follows, and consistency will create and rapidly build momentum.

I am so excited you have chosen to allow me to make this journey with you. If you want continued support on your journey, follow me on YouTube or subscribe to my podcast, Dream Cast. You can also visit DeniseWalsh.com for additional resources to help you on your way.

Now, keep up the momentum and continue to dream big!

Made in the USA
Monee, IL
01 February 2023